Intere

C000149000

Convers

How to Always Have Something to Say

By

Paul Kembly

Copyright

the Publisher is provided beforehand. Any additional rights reserved.

Furthermore, the information that can be found within the pages described forthwith shall be considered both accurate and truthful when it comes to the recounting of facts. As such, any use, correct or incorrect, of the provided information will render the Publisher free of responsibility as to the actions taken outside of their direct purview. Regardless, there are zero scenarios where the original author or the Publisher can be deemed liable in any fashion for any damages or hardships that may result from any of the information discussed herein.

Additionally, the information in the following pages is intended only for informational purposes and should thus be thought of as universal. As befitting its nature, it is presented without assurance regarding its prolonged validity or interim quality. Trademarks that are mentioned are done without written consent and can in no way be considered an endorsement from the trademark holder.

Table of Contents

Introduction

I remember days when I would spend an entire day with my friends and barely say a single word. I remember how I would sit with my family during dinner and listen to what everybody got to say, quiet, until someone asked me a question directly. I remember days when having a conversation was something special, not because I didn't have an opportunity to speak, but because I had to spend so much time thinking what to say. Now it is almost funny to think back to those days, days when I would spend half an hour before sending a text message to a friend. I used to wonder if I should use different words, or if I should wait for a better time.

I never thought about it as a problem, in some way I was comfortable with it, but mostly I just didn't know any better. Now with all the freedom and lightness that comes from my social skills, I am just wondering how could I wait for so long? how could I settle for something so grey? as life without freedom in self-expression.

There is nothing wrong with being introverted, being comfortable with silence and enjoying quality me time. I see great power in silence, but in silence by choice, silence because you choose it, not because you have no choice. This choice gives you freedom, gives you an opportunity to decide. Whether you want to have a conversation with a stranger or a laugh with a colleague, you are free to choose and this freedom feels damn good.

This book is about conversations to have, about questions to ask, and ideas to discuss. This book is about you developing skills necessary to express yourself into the world. Forget about sitting in silence with a blank stare, while your mind is desperately searching for a single word to say at least something. Imagine a life where gender or status of a person in front of you doesn't affect you. Imagine you can speak with your friends about your deepest secrets and your colleagues coming over to have a chat with you, just because you are fun to chat with.

All this is closer than you think it is.

Whether you are just looking for a few dinner table topics or starting your journey to build social skills, welcome and enjoy.

Paul.

Instructions

This book is divided into four parts: theory, preps and gimmicks, exercises and advanced steps.

The first part should help you to understand what is a good topic, what is a bad topic and how you can use it to thrive in social situations. Information is to help you understand communication on a deeper level, so when you are thinking what should I say next, what can we talk about? You can use those knowledges to build a topic, come up with a question or construct a case. It is written to provide you with insight into what is going on behind the scene in daily communications. This should draw your attention to mind blocks, limiting beliefs or some mistakes you do that are limiting your ability to speak freely with anyone. Understanding what exactly is stopping you and what to do about it should help you bring a permanent and deep change in how you express yourself, improving your social skills.

The second part is filled with actual examples, topics, questions and various gimmicks to use straight away. So, if you are just looking for an emergency button, something to just throw into the silence, grab one throw, see where it will lead to. This is however a temporary solution, this may help you assess the situation on the spot, but you can't rely on the list of question and topics for ever. What you should do with this, is to read through them, find what works best for you, remember those or write them down to have them ready for you to use when you need them. There is no need to remember all of them. Choose a few you like, apply them, see if they work for you and then experiment with others. Also be creative and resourceful, adjust them to suit your needs.

The third part contains exercises to practise at home in your spare time. This is a very important part of this book, as it will help you to really understand information and learn how to come up with things to say on the spot. This will also help you understand what topics and strategies are working best for you. This will give you long-lasting results and actually develop skills that will help you to become free and flexible in your communications and expressions. You will need to use knowledge from part one and various examples from part two to learn how to create your own preps, to be a perfect fit for your needs. Doing those exercises will develop your creative thinking, ability to come up and switch topics, speak for longer without running out of things to say and naturally flow through conversation.

The fourth part will provide you with advises and advance steps that will require you to go out of our comfort zone, challenge yourself in order to get results that will not just make you better at speaking, but will develop your personality. Having something to say is just a small part of being good at conversations. Some people say," it not what you say but how you say it that matters." This part of the book will help you develop qualities necessary for speaking with confidence, freedom and power.

Part 1 Theory

Chapter One Mind Set
You can speak with anyone on any topic.

Few years back, when I was studying charisma and trying to understand how some people are popular with everyone in the room, while other people like me are only popular with few friends. I came to a realisation it is all about how you speak to people and what you say to them. While I was careful doing inside jokes with my friends, and keeping my personal stories away from a large group, popular people didn't.

Then it hit me. The reason I was popular with some people, the reason it was so easy to speak with some people and difficult to speak with others, was my mindset. Somewhere deep inside my head I had decided that I can share some stories with some people, while I considered other people strangers, and I spoke with them like with strangers. We spoke about generic topics, small talk that didn't bond us in any way. It was boring and impressionless. When you speak to people you just met in this way, this is how they see you, what they think about you they give you what you give them. If I just met you and you speak about boring topics, I will assume that you are boring, because I only know things about you that you display to me. This realisation made a profound difference in my social life and personal life once I implemented the same principle.

This is became a powerful tool in all my social interactions, as now when I meet people, I know that their reaction is feedback on how I am speaking to them. This will not be the case with everyone, but a general rule of thumb. Do the best you can to make communication easy, friendly, and informal. Share information about you, that will show real you, feelings, fears, this will give a person a better idea of dynamic and relationship that is developing between you.

Everyone is your friend

Remember this: Don't worry about being smooth. Feeling of awkwardness, that there is something wrong, that you have to do something special - it is all in your head. Your prejudices and beliefs create walls in your mind that make you think that with some people you can speak about anything, while with others you have to be selective with your topics. It is true only to an extent of your comfort, and what you feel comfortable will change with time.

Best way to get out of your head when you want to start an effective conversation with someone, with whom you don't have that much confidence – imagine he or she is your best friend. Don't rush, spend some time here, reflect on it, think about how you speak with your best friends. All those topics can be transferred into conversations with strangers, but you just don't have the same level of comfort. Maybe there is a fear of judgment or fear of being misunderstood, but this is nothing more than a mental wall. People who are comfortable with whom they are and own what they do, have no problems telling strangers their opinions, share personal stories or even fears.

Take some time and think about how you interact with different people from different social backgrounds. Friends, family, colleagues, lovers, depends on what they know about you and what you want them to think about you, tell them different stories, and show them your different sides. This is especially noticeable thing to go through with new people in your life. We tend to overthink what is normal, allowed, or how we want to be perceived. By just thinking about a person in front of you as of your best friend, you will destroy mental barriers and will make conversation so much more natural, that it will amaze you.

Social skills

As someone who spend most life quiet, observing how people speak so freely and socialise without any barriers, I failed to notice that world is full of people just like me. The world is actually full of people who don't know when it is their turn to speak or what they should say. This is an important piece of information you need to keep in mind when you socialise with someone you just meet. You need to consider that it may be as difficult for them to find something to say as it is for you. It is really easy to overlook, a person in front of you can be freaking out and desperately trying to come up with something to say, while on the surface seem cool, maybe even a little bored.

As someone who is making a conscious effort to develop social skills and master conversation, you should always try to take this responsibility on your shoulders. Once you start seeing things from this perspective, it is not you against the world; it is you out there to save the world. Do everything you can to make it easier for others to speak with you. Listen carefully when someone is speaking; this will encourage them to speak more. Ask relevant questions; this will show that you are paying attention. Share your opinions, thoughts and stories; it will provide more material to speak about.

I have noticed that among people who are struggling with conversation, there are people who are comfortable with silence and there are people who are too lazy to put an effort into conversation. There is nothing wrong with either of them, you may be one of those people yourself, I used to be both. What it means, however, is that you will have to put a bit of work if you want to get a conversation going. The best thing you can do is to make it simple and safe for them to speak to you.

Make it easy to speak with you

It is always a good practice to start a conversation with a question, this will give your companion opportunity to speak. Success of this manoeuvre will greatly depend on a person you speak with, if they are extraverted a single question will get them going. If he happened to be introvert or has poor social skills your question may get short boring answer, no matter how well elaborated question is. People with poor social skills are naturally good a killing conversation. In this case, you should be ready to do the work. When you ask a question, you put the responsibility of coming up with conversation material on another person. If their social skills are not that strong, this can be a challenging task, so after you are given an opportunity to speak, be ready to bring up easy to speak topic. Don't be afraid to spend some time talking, it may take a few minutes for a person to get out of their head and tune into conversation.

Refer to the chapter on small talk to get a better insight on how to start a casual conversation. Also, if after a few minutes you see that person doesn't respond positively, let it go. It is a good practice to speak with everyone you can, as it will develop your social skill greatly, but don't think it is your duty. Do your best to start a conversation and if you see that someone doesn't want to talk, don't molest them. With time, as your skill will develop, you will notice that more and more people respond positively to your attempts to speak to them.

Chapter Two Questions

Questions are the easiest way to start a conversation; however, there are a few tricks to keep a conversation going after. There are few draw back with question – they put pressure of conversation on another person. So, in a situation where a person you are speaking with is struggling to keep the conversation going, or has no interest in it at all, you are throwing him the ball and waiting for results. In this scenario, it is very common to get answers that go nowhere, answers not designed to keep a conversation going. The best way around it is asking open-ended question and opinions, this will push a person to give a longer answer and provide more material for conversation.

There is nothing people like more than speaking about themselves, so if you can get the conversation personal and connect to their passion and interest, you are all sorted. However, you need to be careful not to bombard a person with questions, as it will just create pressure and can raise suspicion. Even if you are speaking with a friend or your partner throwing one question after another will bring a lot of attention to the way you are communicating. This may raise suspicion, like you are searching for something – questioning them.

In order to avoid this don't just bombard person with questions, and if after two questions the conversation doesn't flow – take the lead. A question is already a conversation topic. When you ask a question – you propose a topic, so if a person didn't get hooked, try to explore and develop the topic yourself. Sometimes people just need a bit of extra information to understand what you mean. Give a few comments about the question; you will make it easier for a person to answer it or start a discussion. In many cases, direct question, especially if it is more complex and aimed to lead into a deep conversation, will be overwhelming. So, if you don't get a good long answer, something that is a solid conversation material – answer this question yourself. This should provide enough information for another person, create more comfort and help them to develop the topic.

One thing I want to draw your attention to is that there are a lot of people who are very clumsy with expressing their ideas and opinions. The fact that someone can speak a lot doesn't make them particularly good at expressing well how they feel or what they think about more complex topics. It is like an interview question that you haven't prepared for. That's why I advise you to pick a few questions that you like more questions that resonate with you and before taking in on the streets, answer them yourself. This way, if you are met with a confused stare or dead-end answer, you can lead the conversation.

Chapter Three Debating

Debating is just a fancy word for arguing. This something that your girlfriend or boyfriend is doing when they are coming up with a long list of things of why it was your fault. Coming up with evidences and trying to prove their point of view. That leads to you stating your case, your point of view, arguments to support your claim, that leads into a passionate argument about who is right and who is sleeping on the sofa tonight.

We are going to use the process described above to construct a case. You can use this technique to build more complex topic that will engage people in conversation. Few guide lines to follow is if you are going to do this with people who are outside your close circle: it is better to construct a case about more neutral topics don't make it personal. Don't get offended or emotional, this is exactly how things get out of control and debate becomes an argument. Some people associate themselves too much with topics, they take close to heart and lose control when their opinion is met with opposing arguments. This is something that you should be aware of in yourself first of all. Remember: passionate speaking is good; it adds colours and dimensions to your speech, getting emotional and losing control will make you a drama queen.

This is something you may notice if you think back to some of your previous arguments or verbal conflicts you had. When conversation went in a completely different direction. And even through you were right with your initial point, you lost the argument because another person managed to overcome your logic and lead you into a conversational trap. This is something you can learn to deal with, you can develop a sharp attention to where conversation is going and if information presented is relative to what you are speaking about. To develop necessary skills, it is better to use a organised system and rules in the beginning.

Starting a debate

As formal as it may sound, debate doesn't have to be. I think the best approach is to see it as something in between an actual argument and formal debate. A well-structured discussion about a selected topic. It would be a good idea to explain your friends what are you up to. Experienced debater can come up with strong arguments, supported with facts and logic; he can see when arguments he or she is presented with are valid or invalid. When you are just starting out, and your perception is not that sharp, fast stream of opinions and facts that are remotely connected to the topic can throw you off, get confused, and make you feel like a person in front of you know what they are talking about.

Explain your friends that you would like to practise debating, that you would like them to prove you wrong on a selected topic. It is better not to rush and think carefully about what you will say as well as analyse what other person will say. See it as a chess game, play carefully and think about your moves.

Claim

Claim is the first step of discussion. This can be as short as a few words or as long as a paragraph. It is a statement, opinion it is something that you want to prove and disprove.

1. Red colour improves sales.
2. Orange juice is good for your health.
3. The death penalty will reduce crime rates.
4. Drinking alcohol can have both negative and positive effects on one's life. Moderate drinking can be beneficial.
5. Active sports often lead to injuries. Injuries will reduce quality of your life more, than benefit you can get from doing sports. It is better not to do sports.

Claim should make clear which side are you taking, in support or gains the statement. You can discuss pretty much anything, but it is better to work with topics you have some level of expertise or knowledge. This will help with next steps– arguments and evidences. Without any related knowledge, those are going to be weak and vague.

Arguments

Arguments are what you are going to use to support your claim. Those are the reasons why side you have taken is the right side; This is why you are right and who ever tries to prove you are wrong is wrong. You should select clear and easy-to-understand arguments, they should not be sending your listeners and or opponents in some unknown direction. The goal of debate is to convince others to take you side in discussion. So, your arguments should be easy to understand, reasonable and relatable.

When you are presenting arguments, you don't just say: That's why I am right. You want to make sure that people know what are you talking about, use common language and examples. Right arguments don't just support your claim, they change opinions through sound logic. You do want to use emotions do add an edge to your arguments, show to your listeners that you are not the enemy. By being relatable you make it easier for others to accept your side, but those should never be the core of your arguments. It may make your argument appear stronger than they are, that means your opponent can use it against you.

Evidence

Evidence is something to back up your arguments. As mentioned above, it is better to choose a topic you are familiar with, as you want to be able to prove what are you saying. Valid evidences are well-known facts, authority in a field opinion, research data. Evidence should prove that your arguments are true. Invalid evidence are personal opinions, feeling, and unchecked data. If I tell you that orange juice is good for your health, because my mother told so, unless my mother is a doctor, nutritionist or has some level of related expertise this is a weak argument.

To succeed in debate, you want to present strong arguments and back them up with a proof. On the other hand you want to find a weakness in argument presented by your opponent and question their evidences.

Conclusion

Conclusion is where you sum up everything in one easy to chew piece. You want to analyse incongruences in what your opponent has parented and bring up your strongest points. Here you want to explain why your arguments matter and how things are connected.

Using this you can present your friends or companions with a statement or a case and invite them for discussion to prove you are wrong, or just to practise your argumentation skills. Some people love to argue, that is the part of their nature, for others it is a big challenge. Constructing a solid case will require an organized thinking and practice; however, it is a valuable skill to have that will be useful in all areas of your life. Practicing constructing cases will develop your negotiation skills and will help to defend yourself from verbal attacks. With a bit of time and practice you will learn to notice weaknesses in the arguments that people are using against you, as well as coming up with better arguments yourself.

Chapter Four Speaking about what you like vs what they like

Finding similarities is an extremely powerful tool to succeed in any communication; That's why you should always try to find topics that will work for both of you. Speaking about a topic you both know will provide you both with material to speak and will give an opportunity to go in-depth and explore specific details. It will also show that you are alike, this will form a bond and create trust. All that said, it is not always obvious what are your similarities and if you have anything you can use to connect at all.

In those cases, it makes sense trying to explore if your conversational partner likes any of your topics. Leading a conversation with what you enjoy and find interesting, this should provide you with plenty of material to speak about. Sometimes you will need to go on for a few minutes before you manage to hook your speaking partner. Unless he or she really doesn't want to speak with you, they just need something to catch their attention. In such cases, don't be afraid to develop a topic you like, tell your favourite story and see if a person will have something to say.

Problem with speaking about what you like is that you can get carried away and speak about something that no one else cares about, without giving them a chance to change a topic or participate in conversation. Same goes for opposite scenario, when your companion gets to do the same. This can be a fairly difficult experience, to deal with a person who just can't stop speaking and can happen even when you share a common topic. Important thing to remember is to make a few seconds pauses here and there, to give other person an opportunity to get involved.

Advice: when dealing with people who just never stop talking - be straight forward about it. There is a really important rule of communication you will see again and again – <u>you can say anything you want, as long as you are being respectful.</u> Don't be rude, don't tell others to shut up, but if you are in the room with a person, and for the last 10 minutes you have just been listening to what they got to say, maybe it is a time to take action. Don't be rude, just let another person know that they got carried away and you want to say something.

Speaking about what they like is a great strategy to use with people who are not in the mood for conversation. If a person just doesn't seem to be reactive to anything you say, getting them speaking about something they care about is a great way to get the ball rolling. Sometimes people need some time to warm up towards you. Getting them to speak about what they like and care about will bring positive emotions and excitement that is connected to the topic. When you will feel that ice is broken, redirect conversation, if that particular topic doesn't work for you.

When it comes to discovering topic he or she cares about, you will need to pay attention to their reaction. If a person is giving you a cold shoulder but responds to some words or comments, move in that direction. This will require careful listening and full attention, but all of those skills are extremely valuable and will improve your social skills greatly.

Chapter Five What not to speak about

As I've mentioned before, you can speak about anything you want, as long as you speak with respect. In many situations, acceptable topics will be decided by settings – people, situation, etc. There is no borderline on how far a conversation can go in a company of a best friends or behind the closed doors of the bedroom. However, with everyday social situations, you should follow few guidelines, this will make your life easier and will give you a chance to form a better connection with people. Once you get to know each other on a deeper level and connection is made - explore those topics.

The reason behind this is that when you meet someone for the first time, they don't have a formed opinion about you. People tend to jump to conclusions really fast and then interpret situation based on those conclusions. With topics that evoke strong emotions in people, topics that they care about a lot, this can be a sharp unconscious reaction. Something you consider being a joke can become a statement or insult, just because your conversational partner doesn't know your communication style.

Complaining

Without a doubt discussing your problems is important. Your friends and family care about you and you should share difficulties you are going through with people who can support you. However, going around telling people how bad things are will not make things better. Complaining is a projection of your problems into other people, it is a negative form of interaction that burdens listener. Complaining in a social situation, especially with people you don't know well, will create an impression that you are a negative person with a bunch of problems. This will push people away from you or will surround you with people who enjoy complaining. You don't want any of those things.

Medical and Personal Issues

You do want to share personal information, telling people about yourself and what you do. Sharing promotes sharing, but there are certain things people don't want to know about you. Difficult information regarding your personal life and medical condition can make people feel uneasy. Once again, if they don't know you well, they may misjudge a situation. They may feel like you need comforting or help, or advice. In cases when you do need help, speak with right people who know you and have appropriate knowledge. Last thing you want is advice from a stranger who don't know anything about you and your condition.

Gossips and speaking bad behind people's backs

Gossiping can be a big temptation; I am always curious to learn new things. However, I always pay attention to who is saying it, as this is the person who can't be trusted. The same goes to speaking bad about others. The moment people learn that you have those traits, they will always associate them with you. On top of that, things can backfire, rumours can lead back to you, with all the consequences.

Lies

This one once again is coming down to trust. Once people stop believing you, your words will lose value. Lying is also perceived to be manipulative, so people may start to think that you are perusing a personal agenda and have hidden motives behind your words. Unlike other topics that you can go into with your friends, lying is something you should avoid amongst your friends first of all.

Religion and Politics

All-time favourite. I personally find this to be a remarkable material for conversations. There are just so many directions you can take it, only problem is people tend to get overprotective about their opinions when it comes to these two topics. If you can't stay ice cold and speak about politics and religion for the sake for conversation, you probably shouldn't go down that path.

Chapter Six Conversation types
Small talk

Small talk gets a lot of bad fame through the nature of how plain and boring it can get. This classic conversation about the weather, or any other question that you have answered 3 times today. Usually this kind of conversation are there to get a read of pressure that silence creates. It becomes especially obvious when you get stuck in a room or bump into a person who you know in person yet, there is nothing that connects you. Now you are going to spend some time together and you can't just stay silent, you are not strangers, you should have a chat. This leads to those I don't really care about what to ask and what to say conversation. This kind of conversation that leads nowhere and will not make any difference if you had it in the first place.

Unless you said something really stupid and now, this person will have this impression about you.

However, the empty nature of this type of conversation is a reflection of social skills of people involved. Small talk can be a powerful tool in making the first impression and building your social circle as well as acquiring valuable connections. You see, when you just met someone for the first time, or have just a few minutes in the elevator, you don't want to be discussing complex matter. There is a time and place to speak about those things, however you can still have a good chat about in a span of just 5 minutes. Small talk is your way to make a first impression and take conversation further if you want to or need to.

So how can you do that?

First: Avoid boring questions that lead nowhere.

Second: Don't rush into answering a question you have being asked.

Many people consider it to be obligatory to answer questions, they are afraid to come across as rude, but with small talk you can be flexible. Reason behind it is small talk is there to fill in the void, it should be more fun than silence, so if you make conversation better by answering a different question or redirection of the conversation you win the round. (ten points to the Gryffindor!) If you feel like a person just asking a question, to fill the gap make a favour to both of you by redirecting it!

Example:

-So, you come here often?

-I just remembered the story __ told me, is that true that you did ___?

Associations, funny memory, you can throw literally anything. In exercise section, you will find exercise to help you jump from topic to topic, on the fly. If a person really wants to know the answer, they will ask you again and then you can answer. You can always say something like sorry I missed that.

Make a complement and build on it

This is something that you may want to prepare in advance, but having even one line will last you a lifetime. The way it works is people love to speak about themselves and about their things. By directly addressing a quality or item they possess will immediately make them feel special and excited that you noticed it. This will raise excitement and energy in conversation. Straight after that add WHY, don't just say I like your ring, you'll get thank you! Game over, you just lost the round.

Example: I Love your ring; I had a similar one I bought in Bangkok.

Here you give an opportunity to a person to speak about them if they would like to speak about a ring. Or you give them an opportunity to speak about your trip to Bangkok. Give them a chance to select a topic they like; this will make conversation engaging and natural. Quality of your why will greatly influence conversation. You will find more examples and exercises in second and third part of the book.

Make an assumption

This works well on its own and if you bump into a curious person or someone who is easily impressed you don't need anything else. However best execution of this move will be to mix it up with complement strategy described above.

All you need to do is make an assumption about a person:

You look like you know how to fight.

You look like you know how to stir a martini.

Something tells me you play guitar.

You don't need to be right and coming up with more obnoxious assumptions will give you a bonus. Try to stay on a positive side, assume "cool" traits and qualities. This way a person will feel flattered and curious about what has made you think that. This will lead them into asking you questions, so have something good ready. You will have more examples and tips in the chapter with gimmicks.

The goal of small talk is to get to know one another and to arrive to a topic that you both will enjoy. So, it's a good idea raise the energy and make an interesting conversation, rather than generic. Make it: light, fun and personal, that's all you need to do.

Every day interactions

Most of your daily conversations are going to fit into this group. Conversations with your friends, family members, partners, colleagues and most common daily situations. There is a big chance that the reason you got this book is because you are looking for a conversational material in daily life and in casual situations. Regular conversation almost has no rules. All you need to do is feel free and confident too approach topics that you would like to speak on. In further chapters you will find everything you need to master daily conversations and never run out of things to say. In this chapter we will cover just few things.

In the same way as with small talk there are few dos and don'ts that will improve your conversation.

Take responsibility for conversation

Think about what you can do so people can talk to you. Generally, what you want to do is follow the Small Talk guidelines, aim for a light and fun conversation, but here you have opportunity to go deeper, develop interesting topics and form deeper connections. A great t way to build a connection with someone is to share personal information, such as talking about family. Family is really an easy topic to bring up and it opens doors to speak about feelings and relationships.

To make conversation interesting and form a stronger connection with a person, you should try to move further away from surface general conversation and move toward feelings. Things like desire, dreams and fears will get people speaking about things that they actually care about. Family is a great way to get a conversation going in this direction as you can simply say: I love/hate/miss my brother and lead the conversation to why this is the case. You can do this exact same step with topics like friends or work. Don't let it become a boring conversation about what do you do? Ask for motivation behind it, as how that makes them feel.

You may notice that some people will get confused when asked about how do they feel about their job, or give you a vague answer. It may be because no one ever talks about it, so they don't have much practice in expressing those thoughts or they don't feel as comfortable sharing it just yet. In either case, always be ready to share your side of the story, speak about your feelings and dreams. This will provide them with example, if they need it and extra material to speak about. If they don't want to speak about themselves, then you probably need to create more comfort, once they get to know you better, they will be ready to share with you.

Hight Energy vs Intensity.

Generally, you want to stay in high energy in your daily interaction, this will make your communication easy going and light. it will also express friendliness and invite people to open up. Everyone loves energy and naturally attracted to people who project it. However, even if you don't have that level of enthusiasm in any one given moment, you can still effectively express yourself and have interesting and engaging conversation.

When it comes to high energy communication you are loud, outgoing, you can be silly – you are in the mood. This is a great state to be in and great state to lead conversation from as you don't take things too seriously, generally easy going and flexible with what you have to say. High energy means fun.

High intensity focuses that energy in one direction. You can associate high intensity with a strong eye contact, active listening and strong feeling of presence. When a person you are speaking with is only paying attention to what you got to say. This can be overwhelming for some people, not everyone is comfortable under pressure that intense attention can produce.

Depending on where the conversation is going to you will need to adjust accordingly. If you are moving towards more complex and important topics – deep conversation, you want to tune down your energy and focus on what your partner has to say. This will show that you are taking the matter seriously and are ready for discussion. On the other hand, if you are trying to make conversation fun and entertaining, want to make people laugh or just have fun, raising energy is a better move. People will mimic your behaviour when you are speaking to them and will get serious or excited depending on what state you are projecting.

Fun chat

This is the fun bit of conversation, banter, bullshit talk, conversation full of jokes. Having a fun and engaging conversation will charge you with energy and will definitely brighten up your day. laughing is a strong bonding experience and if you can form connection based on fun and high energy people will keep coming back to you. The human nature is such that we love fun, we are addicted to dopamine our brain produces when we are having fun.

Sense of humour is a big and complicated topic, developing it requires creativity and a lot of work, but there are few principles that will make you instantly fun and easy to speak with straight away. Those are:

Enthusiasm

Be excited to see people, raise your voice, smile go as far as doing something silly.

Expressing excitement will show whoever you are about to speak with, that you are happy to see them and you are in a playful mood. That will make them mimic your energy level and prepare for fun and playful interaction straight away. In some cases, this will be enough.

Don't filter yourself

Don't worry about what you are going to say, just go with the flow, fun interactions mean jokes, silly conversations, overall sense of freedom and comfort with who you are and what you do. What you think is funny, is not always going to match with the company you are in, don't worry about this. Just focus is on expressing yourself.

Don't get offended

When it comes to banter and throwing jokes back and forth you may feel like people picking on you, don't take it seriously. If you are playing – play, there is always a chance that someone will take a joke too close to the heart, but don't be that person. In the same manner don't try to make jokes at someone else's expense as this can lead to verbal conflict rather then friendly banter.

Time and place

I am a strong believer that in most of your daily conversation you should be on a funny side. If not, cracking jokes left and right, you should at least try to keep energy of a conversation on a high end. This will lead to having a higher emotional state and better mood. It will make it easier for you to flow between topics and will attract people to you. However, you don't want to become a person whom no one is taking seriously.

Deep conversation

Your ability to have a deep and meaningful conversation will become your most powerful tool in developing relationships with people around you. This will give you an ability to speak with someone for a few hours and form a level of connection that could usually take years to form. This is your ability to speak about things that matter, fragile topics like relationships, fears, weaknesses, hopes and dreams. Those topics don't tend to surface naturally as they require certain settings, you need to have some level of comfort with whoever you are speaking with and someone has to take a first step.

Sharing first can be extremely difficult, it requires bravery and confidence. Like telling someone that you love them for the first time, giving away a secret that will make you vulnerable and fragile. You will know you are on the right path, when you feel like you want to stop and return to safety of your comfort zone. Like with any other skill you can develop, become good and master at it and enjoy all the benefits and positive changes it will bring into your life.

This will also require a good setting, you shouldn't just jump into speaking about your deepest desires, even if you are comfortable doing this. Meaningful conversation is a progression of a conversation, next step in your relationship with a person. You should stick to high intensity when you are having a meaningful conversation. This will show the person you are speaking with that you care about what they got to say.

Sharing

Once you form a connection and feel comfortable with a person, to start deep conversation, someone has to share first. Since you are reading this book, it's going to be you. It is better to start sharing from positive spectre of emotions, like your dreams, hopes, wishes, and passions. This should create a strong base and build more trust and comfort between you. From there, you can move on to more difficult topics like fears, weaknesses and failures. Sharing your secrets and showing a side of you that is normally hidden will create an immense amount of trust, that will inspire another person to share as well.

There will be situations when whoever you are speaking with won't be ready to share. Sometimes it will take a nudge. In those cases you can use phrases like: I don't know if you ever felt this way or did that ever happen to you? It is important not to be pushy, your actions don't oblige anyone to share back, they create a safe space for sharing. Some people will need more time and comfort than others. If you will keep pushing a person to open up through a deep conversation technique, people may start to think that you are trying to interrogate them.

Listening

Starting to share can be a liberating experience and a sensation of relief can make you want to keep going. However, you need to give some space for other person to share and you need to pay careful attention to what they got to say. Starting a deep conversation and not listening to what your partner has to say will show them that you don't care about what they got to say. This will make them take a step back and bring their guard up.

Listening is probably most important step in deep conversation, as only by listening carefully you will be able to understand what a person in front of you is really talking about, what are their fears or what do they really want to express.

Relate

Don't just listen to start speaking again. This will show that you don't really care about what a person has to say, you just want to speak. Find similarities in your stories, relate to feelings and emotions described. This will show that you understand and form strong bond that will help you both to feel comfortable and confident to share further. Meaningful conversations will form a strong bond with friends and will improve a connection with people you love. Once you start having those conversations, you will let people know that they can have this type of conversation with you. After the first initial step of sharing is done and ice is broken, in the future, they are more likely to take the first step.

Chapter Seven What actually gives freedom in communication

Confidence

In short, confidence is a faith in yourself. This is how much you trust that you can handle the situation, this is how much you believe in yourself. Confidence is not a fixed trait and can be developed or broken by events in your life. Confidence greatly affects everything you do, including your ability to express yourself.

Low confidence can lead to self-doubt and fear of action, as we may question our ability to handle consequences of our actions. This is important as on a closer examination you may realise that this is what is stopping you from being as expressive and verbal as you would like to. The biggest barrier we have that stops us from being as flexible with some people is this fear of how people will react to what we will say. Will this offend them? Will it ruin our image? Will it change the dynamic of your relationships? All this is just a mind game. It may come in a different shape and form, depending on if you are speaking to your loved one, your parents or someone at work.

Freedom in interactions comes from confidence, it comes from not worrying about what people will think about what you are saying. It doesn't mean you don't care about what people will think about your words, it means you are willing to be heard and face the consequences of your words.

This may sound a bit taunting, but notice that in your daily conversation with friends you are careless and free in your expressions as you are not afraid that your words can offend someone, or affect your reputation. In conversations with opposite gender, however, you tend to be more selective with what you got to say. In most cases, we do it unconsciously to create a better impression. Probably same things happens with colleagues and acquaintances. Desire to preserve or create a certain image of ourselves and not come across as weird, puts limitations on what we feel comfortable talking about.

However, if you want to reach your full social potential, you must leave this mindset behind. You have to be willing to take risk, bring up all kinds of topics and speak up your mind, to develop confidence and freedom in communication. Remember, you can say anything as long as you are being respectful. If you pay close attention to charismatic people around you, you may notice that not every joke they do is funny, not every conversation goes smoothly. However, those people don't get concerned with those little things. You shouldn't either.

You should stop worrying about fitting in every group and being accepted by everyone, instead you should start speaking your mind and expressing the real you. This may push away some people, but that will also attract people to you. You will naturally get surrounded by the right people, people who share your ideas and understand you. This will make your life better.

Knowledge

Knowledge is power. Nothing will give you as much freedom and confidence in conversation as extensive knowledge and deep understanding of a topic. Knowledge will provide you with material for long monologue if there will be necessity for it. Knowledge of a subject will provide you with countless possibilities for conversation with people who share subject with you. Strong knowledge of a topic will help you to speak with conviction and authority.

It may seem like a mission to develop in-depth knowledge about something, but in reality, this can be done with just 15 minutes a day. We are living in magical times with almost unlimited information in free access, this makes studying extremely accessible. Even if you are not a big fan of reading, which I doubt, since you bought this book, you can use YouTube to get strong insight in almost any subject, by watching documentaries or listening to podcasts.

Now the only thing that you need to do is to choose a subject which should be based on your necessities. If you know that, you have an event on the way that will be focusing on a particular subject, or you are going on a date with a writer, spend some time reading or listening about related subject at home. Just fifteen minutes will provide you enough information to ask relevant questions and build connections with your favourite subject. Imagine this as a preparation for work interview. Great thing about this is that knowledge will stay with you and will accumulate with time. This will greatly expand your overall knowledge and will slowly make you a well-rounded person capable of speaking about literally anything.

Another interesting aspect about knowledge is that even if you know just a little more than a person in front of you,

you can come across as an expert in your field, if you speak with confidence and use the right vocabulary. You will be surprised how many people around us have literally no idea what they are talking about. Even through you can use it to get some extra authority, I would advise you to be careful with speaking a lot about things that you know little about.

Passion

Passion will bring life to your words, add colours and emotions. Strong emotional connection with the topic will let you express yourself with an unprecedented level of expressiveness and the best thing about it, it will be natural. When topic at hand is something we really care about, we tend to forget about all those mental barriers and just go. Opinions, ideas and dreams all go into the mix and leave no space of overthinking.

It is always exciting to listen to passionate speakers, as they tend to be expressive and deliver information through various mediums. Passion turns speaker into a performer. All that said, not everyone can be equally passionate when speaking about their hobbies or even things that matter to them a lot. Some of us are simply not that expressive or emotional. Well, I have good news for you, just like any other skill you can develop ability to speak with passion.

Passionate speaking is considered to be an advanced skill in public speaking and storytelling, but you shouldn't be concerned with that. Being passionate means being real, raw, expressing how you feel about whatever you are talking about. This is charming and fascinating to hear and see. I have a friend who is really passionate geologist, I could never imagine that lecture about rocks can be so exciting.

When it comes to passionate speaking, you can work with both high energy and high intensity, the difference is if that high energy will convey happiness and excitement for the topic, while high intensity will convey importance and will make it more intimate. Hight energy will generally be more entertaining. So if you want to share something fun like a funny story or your recent success, high energy, passionate speaking will infect people with energy and excitement. However, if you want to focus attention on something serious, speak about your relationships or issues that you care deeply about, high intensity passionate speaking will underline importance and seriousness.

I think that the best way to develop passionate speaking is to observe it, listen to passionate speaker on YouTube, look for best speeches in the history and try to replicate them. Your body and mind will react to what you say and how you behave, so the moment you start expressing strong emotions you will get a chemical boost that will make you feel intense emotions. Remember that feeling. After doing this few times, you will become familiar with that state and it will be easier to get into it.

Another thing you can do is imagine intense emotions, excitement or anger. Use your body language to support this process. If you want to feel happiness – smile, shout, dance or clap, If you want to feel anger – clinch your fists, put on a grim face expression. You will notice really fast how different you feel yourself. Practice telling a story or a short speech in different states. This will develop your ability to switch emotional states and will make it easier to do it in the future. Repeating this exercise should make you naturally more expressive and once you put some work into it, it will stay with you. With time, it will become effortless to speak with intense emotion, because your body and mind will be used to it on the experiential level.

Part 2 Preps

Chapter Eight Questions Preps

Conversation dies when no one has anything to add to it. The best way to provoke another person to share is to prove them that you can be trusted, that you will understand and won't judge. Most effective way to do it is by sharing first. Be sincere, show that you are real and feel comfortable speaking about the topic. Answer in advance every question you are going to ask. This way, even if a person doesn't get hooked, you will be ready to lead the conversation. This will provide more topics to speak about. This way, you don't just bombard a person with a question or even if you do, it isn't obvious. The list of questions here is not meant to solve all your conversational problems. Choose questions that you like the most, answer them yourself and develop them.

Guide lines:

- Avoid questions that can be answered yes or no
- Don't just ask questions – speak as well
- Ask opinions
- Ask advices
- Share personal opinions

In the exercise section you will find the exercise that will help you to tailor those questions to your personal style and need. If while going thru the list you feel like it is too basic and cheesy, go straight to that exercise.

Small talk

Here you have a list of go to questions for all kind of situations, work, social gathering formal events. Use the information from the chapter on small talk to bring more colours to those questions. Find a question that suit you best and adjust them to be a perfect fit for the situation. You can also refer to the exercise chapter to get a better idea how to transform questions, to suit your needs.

1. What do you do?
2. What do you like about your job?
3. Is your job what you expected it to be?
4. Do you have siblings?
5. What is the best thing about living here?
6. Do you prefer living in the city or in a countryside?
7. Do you prefer having guests or being a guest?
8. What movies do you prefer?
9. Do you enjoy being away from home when travelling?

10. What do you like the most about this city?

11. What is your favourite movie?

12. What are your plans for the weekend?

13. What do you usually do in your free time?

14. How do you know each other?

15. How was your weekend?

16. Do you ever go to live shows?

17. What's the one spot that I should visit in this city?

18. Do you have any pets?

19. What is your favourite food?

20. What food do you like the least?

21. What's your favourite way to waste time?

22. What is your best failure?

23. What household chore have you never done?

24. What language would you like to learn?

25. What skill would you like to learn?

26. Who would you love to punch in the face?

27. Where is the farthest place you've ever travelled in a car?

28. What will break the Internet?

29. Do you like dancing?

30. Do you come here often?

Every day interactions

When it comes to daily conversations, don't over complete it. Don't think like you have to know someone for x amount of time in order to speak about something. See everyone as your friend and behave like you know them for many years. Even if it feels awkward at first, try to ask them the same questions and bring the same topics that you speak about with your friends.

1. What makes you panic?
2. What was the best day of your life?
3. Why do you think the world has so many religions?
4. What accomplishments are you most proud of?
5. Do you have a role model, someone you would like to be like?
6. What's one of your greatest accomplishments?

7. What would you do if money wasn't a problem?

8. What was the most valuable lesson you have learnt so far?

9. Have you ever been skinny dipping?

10. What is your favourite quote?

11. In the last five years, what new belief or behaviour has benefited your life the most?

12. What is your favourite topic to speak?

13. What would you do, if you knew you will succeed?

14. What fear would you like to overcome?

15. What would you do if you knew you will succeed?

16. What was your worst date?

17. How do you like your coffee?

18. Do you have morning rituals?

19. Do you have a best friend?

20. What's the most beautiful place you've ever been to?

21. What are the top things on your bucket list?

22. What do you want to be remembered for?

23. What is your proudest moment?

24. What is the one most interesting thing you have done?

25. Which book has made the biggest influence on you?

26. What do you think is your best quality?

27. How have your priorities and values changed over time?

28. Who's was your biggest inspiration?

29. If you would write a bestselling book, what would it be about?

30. Why are some people cruel?

Fun Chat

When it comes to just having fun conversation, you have to be open-minded and creative. This type of conversation flows better when you have a certain level of connection, but in reality, you just need to be confident enough to be loose. Those questions are not meant to provide you with useful information; they are meant to provide fuel for a fun conversation that will keep you occupied and entertained.

The best thing to do is not to answer those questions in a direct manner - exaggerate. If you think that the worst way to die is by drowning, imagine what it would be like to trip on melted Ben and Jerry's and fall into a sewer. Create most obnoxious stories and create a space for verbal play, just for shits and giggles.

1. What's your favourite dinosaur?

2. What is the worst way to die?

3. What would you eat if had to eat one thing for the rest of your life?

4. What kind of cult would you start?

5. What conspiracy theories do you believe in?

6. Would you like to be a dragon?

7. What song is your zombie killing soundtrack?

8. If there were no consequences, what would you do?

9. What super power would you like to have?

10. How many first graders could you fight before you become overwhelmed?

11. When you poop in a public toilet do you hover, build a nest, or just sit down?

12. Is there something you believe that most people don't?

13. Where is the best place to hide the bodies?

14. Would you rather time travel to the future or to the past?

15. What colour crayon would you eat, if you had to eat a crayon?

16. What was the most ridiculous lie you have ever told?

17. If you had to, would you eat a cat or a dog?

18. What is the weirdest question you have asked someone?

19. What vegetable would you pick to beat up a kid?

20. Would you rather fight a giant cockroach or an army of little crocodiles?

21. What is the weirdest thing you do, but no one knows?

22. What's a question you'd like to answer, but no one asks?

23. What is the most useless talent?

24. What is the creepiest thing you can say to a stranger?

25. What is the weirdest thing you have seen in someone else's home?

26. What is a soundtrack to your life?

27. Would you rather have a second nose or a third ear?

28. What movie title best describes your life?

29. What is the dumbest way to get injured?

30. What is your most embarrassing sex story?

Dates and Relationship

In this section you will find questions that you can ask your partner or a date. If you have been together for some time and are looking for a way to explore your relationships, those questions should help you to rediscover your partner. Many of those questions will be a perfect fit for people who are just starting dating or having their first date. Those questions are made to help you to understand values and build a connection.

1. What does it mean to have a chemistry?
2. When do you feel most lonely?
3. What's something about you that no one knows?
4. What important lesson did you learn from your parents?
5. Which animal would you be?

6. What weird habit do you have?

7. What should a good relationship provide?

8. What's your favourite way to receive attention?

9. What does love mean to you?

10. Where do you want to live when you retire?

11. How do you want to be remembered?

12. What is your favourite thing that I do?

13. What do you like most that I do in bed?

14. What do you think is the most important thing in the relationship?

15. What's your favourite non-sex activity?

16. What should I do, to make you trust me even more?

17. Which of your personality traits do you want to change?

18. What was your first kiss like?

19. What makes you feel like I'm the one for you?

20. What does good friendship look like to you?

21. What personality traits do you value the most?

22. Do you consider yourself a good friend?

23. Have you ever been heartbroken?

24. What really makes you feel loved?

25. What do you think about monogamy?

26. What does cheating mean to you?

27. How often do you think it is normal to want sex?

28. How do you feel about having children?

29. What do I smell like?

30. Have you ever had your heart broken?

Deep conversation

Deep complex questions will require a good setting. Asking those questions out of the blue can be surprising and probably not going to provide good results. It is true that you can have a deep conversation on the spot; however, this is not the case for everyone. With those questions, I advise you to have a bit of consideration with whoever you are going to ask them. Sharing deep thoughts, fears, feelings and doubts can be difficult for many people, even if you are good friends or a going strong couple.

Be prepared to take the lead if the question does not land.

Don't get discouraged if a person doesn't react with long a descriptive answer.

If after you shared your answer conversation doesn't flow, let it go, move on to the next question or next topic.

1. When was the last time you cried?
2. What scares you the most about the future?
3. What makes you feel weak?
4. What is your biggest regret in life?
5. What do you wish your parents would understand?
6. What are you jealous of in others?
7. Of all the people in your family, whose death would be most disturbing? Why?
8. How do you deal with doubt?
9. What's the hardest thing you've ever been through?
10. If you found out you were going to die tomorrow?
11. What does freedom mean to you?
12. How important is happiness to you?

13. Are you happy with your current experience of life?

14. What's your biggest life goal?

15. How do you deal with your fears?

16. Which is more important: Fear, or hope?

17. Who are three most important people in your life?

18. What is the most significant lesson life has taught you?

19. What was your biggest adventure in life so far?

20. What are the five things that made you who you are?

21. Which place is your sanctuary in this world?

22. Why don't you do the things that harm you?

23. What is the best advice you have received?

24. Are you being true to your values?

25. What would you do if you had no fear?
26. What do you think you should stop doing?
27. What question are you afraid to ask?
28. What is Right and Wrong?
29. What happens after death?
30. When can you break the rules?

Chapter Nine Topics Preps

Literally anything can be a conversation topic, you don't need to overthink it. As your social skill will develop and grow you will learn how to speak about topics that you don't know nothing about while appearing very knowledgeable. All it takes is a bit of practice and confidence in what you say. For now, I am leaving you with a list of easy to go to topics, that you don't need to study or prepare in advance, as they are universal.

Below you will find examples of topics with subtopics. The easiest way to bring up any topic is to ask questions:

Do you like ____?

What is your favourite ____?

It reminds me of ____

From there you can speak about any subtopic you feel like.

Music

Music is one of my favourites go to topics, it is easy to speak about and it can go in many directions. It is really easy to bring up, as even most basic question: What kind of music do you listen to? Is super common and people always react well on it.

However most common answer is: I am listening to a bit of everything. It is not going to help you much, so be prepared to make conversation a bit more interesting. Branch out into more specific topics like:

1. Favourite bands
2. Concerts you have been to
3. Musical instrument you play or would like to learn how to play
4. Video clips
5. Influence music has on your life

6. How music can influence your mood
7. Creating music
8. Music industry
9. Modern music
10. Music genres

Travel

Traveling is another extremely easy topic to speak about. Traveling means holidays and adventures, topics related to traveling can bring up a lot of memories and emotions. This is a good thing as it will raise overall conversation energy.

Once you hit travelling topic you can branch out to:

1. Holidays
2. Summer destinations
3. Winter destinations
4. Backpacking
5. Cruise
6. Hitchhiking

7. Packing luggage
8. How do you feel about planes?
9. Longest bus ride
10. Missing home and family

Food

All offered topics are based on common situations, so they should be easy to go to. You don't need to be a chef or even to know how to cook. In fact, your relationship with food can be a topic on its own. When it comes to speaking about topics all you need to do is express your opinion or any relevant experience. Even if you don't know nothing about cooking, or any other topic, but whoever you are speaking with is really passionate about the topic, you can just ask questions, and they will handle 90% of the work. You can always throw in things like: I never thought about it in this way. Really? Where did you learn that?

Sub topics include:

1. Eating out
2. Cooking at home
3. Allergies
4. Favourite food
5. Deserts
6. Diets
7. Best food
8. Junk food
9. Healthy eating
10. Take away

Books

With Game of Thrones, Harry Potter and Lord of the Rings, books made a strong influence on cinema and modern culture. This should make it easy to move between cinema, cartoons, comics and series. You can even go as far as throwing manga and anime in the mix. Choose whatever is the biggest topic in the present and then lead conversation in preferred direction through association.

1. Your favourite book
2. Studying
3. Book that made most influence on you
4. Movies and series adaptation
5. Importance of reading
6. E book, paper books and audiobooks
7. Writing a book
8. Speed reading
9. Literature
10. Magazines

Partying

If you don't like going out or drinking at all, you still can get a lot out of this topic. Things like Burning Man Festival, Tomorrow Land, Carnival in Rio and Day of the Dead are great way to speak about dreams, your bucket list and everything below.

1. Going out with friends
2. Heavy drinking
3. Socialising
4. Networking
5. Concerts
6. Festivals
7. Birthdays
8. Beer pong
9. Night clubs
10. Theme parties

Sports

I'll be honest here. I don't like football. I just don't find it interesting and my knowledge about it is fairly basic. But people watch football with friends, while drinking beer, I know people bet money on their favourite teams. This is enough to get a conversation going, use whatever knowledge you have about the topic, form connection and speak about next thing.

1. Martial arts
2. Fitness
3. Running
4. Injuries
5. Doping and supplements
6. Gym
7. Sports wear
8. Diet
9. Olympics
10. Losing and gaining weight

Relationships

Just like with a family, this topic is super easy to bring up and everyone can speak about it. And it goes far beyond romantic relationships. You have relationships with your friends, with your parents or your cat. My cat is a bastard that only consumes my resources and ruins furniture. I think we have toxic co-dependency going on.

11. Dating
12. One-night stands
13. Tinder and online dating
14. Monogamy
15. Family
16. Meeting with parents
17. Braking up
18. First love
19. Cheating
20. Long-distance relationships

Chapter Ten Comments and Complements Preps

Opener

Chose an item of closing that you are most interested in, that will add security to your voice and body language. Also don't be shy to touch another person or ask to hold this particular thing you would like to have a closer look. This will break the distance barrier and set a friendlier tone of communication.

1. I love your ring
2. Cool earrings
3. Really interesting watch
4. Great belt
5. This jacket looks really warm
6. Those shoes look heavy
7. I think I have the same bag at home
8. I use to have same t-shirt
9. I like your style
10. Cool glasses

Follow up

1. My dad used to have the same.

2. I gave exact same to my sister on her birthday, she never wears them.

3. In reminds me of one I used to have. I lost it in "any place you have been to" on my holidays.

4. I think I've seen the same in pawnshop.

5. I always wanted to get one, but I don't want to pay that much for a "whatever that thing is"

6. Do you think it was a good investment? I am looking for one, can't decide.

7. You must be very confident to wear something like this.

8. Did you get it for a dollar?

9. I decided I only will get one for myself once I "a goal you want to achieve"

10. Is it plastic?

Mix and match top and bottom to fit your needs and occasion. Experiment with them to find what works best for you. I found that comments about rings and earing never fail in conversation with women, while men really like their beards and watches.

You can and should be playful here if you have opportunity for it. If you see that person wearing expensive watch, ask them if it was on discount, bought from Ali Express or in pawn shop. Do it with a smile and exaggeration, this will invite person to play and laugh with you. If for some reason you don't feel comfortable doing this, give a longer comment with better hooks. (something to grab attention)

Examples:

- I like your style! You must be very confident to were something like this.

- I love your earing! Is it plastic?

- Great belt! Did you get it for a dollar?

Those examples may seem like an insult for some, but think about your interactions with you friends, you always make small jokes and pick on each other. Doing same with people will show them that you are comfortable with them and don't mind a bit of banter. Play with your voice, express shock or over-exaggerate surprise. This will show them that you are just having a laugh. If you prefer something a bit more formal use:

Really interesting watch, I decided that I will only get one for myself once I "a goal you want to achieve"

This will show sincerer admiration in their taste and lead conversation towards dreams.

This approach is not limited to an item of clothing. You can use character traits, achievements, stories or random made up stuff.

1. You look really confident! Have you had a drink?
2. You walk like you know how to dance! I've been doing salsa, I know!
3. That story "name" told me about you... (stay silent and watch them slowly losing it trying to figure out what do you know)
4. Speech you gave was breath-taking! I feel like it takes years to learn how to speak like this.

5. You look like someone who read a lot. I only read food preparation instructions.

6. You look like someone who can throw a kid really far. Teach me how!

7. You must be hitting your head a lot, being this tall.

8. You actually really cool, I don't know why everyone thinks you are boring.

9. With those eyes, you should be a hand model.

10. You smell really nice today!

When it comes to personal traits and sharper jokes, you need to work your way up. It is not just saying a line and getting a result, you need to say it right, you need to say it with a friendly smile or dead serious face. It takes some practice to become natural at it. Starting with personal belongings is a safe way to build your confidence and skills necessary to effectively verbally play with everyone you meet.

Part 3 Exercises

Chapter Eleven Questions Exercises

As I have mentioned above, there is no right and wrong question to ask, it is all about where are you going to take the conversation. It will also depend on your style of communication, confidence and how fast you can think, all this you can develop with practice. Go through the questions and see what you like, choose something that suits your current style of communication, or situation that you are about to face. Are you going on the date? Are you going out with friends? The best thing to do is plan your strategy according to your plans, as there is no such thing as a master key when it comes to communications.

How to work with this list of questions:

Choose a question from the list:

How do you know each other?

Develop it:

The great way to play with this question is to make an assumption about people. This will provide more material to speak about.

Example:

- Are you best friends?
- Are you a couple?
- Are you brothers/sisters/siblings?
- Did you meet during heist?

Turn it into a statement:

You look like you met during a bank robbery.

You can make really obnoxious assumptions about people, play it out, make it fun. This will depend on the settings, but if questions in the examples are too simple and boring for you, this is what you should do. This will invite people to play with you, how effective this will be, will depend on how creative and fun both sides are.

Turning questions into statements is a great way to keep questioning people without drawing too much attention to what you do. If your assumption is correct, they will tell you about it, if no, they will still tell you about it. One way or another it will make them ask why did you assume that, what was that thing that made it obvious or created this impression.

Let's try again.

Question

What Do You Want To Be When You Grow Up?

Develop

Did you want to be a crazy cat lady when you grow up?

Statement

Something tells me that you wanted to become crazy cat lady when you grew up.

Question

What would you do if you won 10 000$?

Develop

Would you be able not to spend everything you won in a lottery on pizza and beer?

Statement

I am sure that if you won 10 000$ in lottery, you would spend it all on pizza and beer.

Do 3 to 5 question for each category.

Chapter Twelve Writing Exercise

Writing is an extremely effective way to develop thinking. This will require a bit of determination from you, but it will produce extremely rewarding results. In order for us to speak well, we need to be able to think clearly, to have our thoughts organised, this way you don't get lost in your own words. Writing will help you organise your thinking; It will show you how much you actually know on the topic and how well you know it.

Apart from developing your thinking, it will improve how effective you are with your vocabulary. Have you ever had a situation when you just can't think of a word or word you use just doesn't mean exactly what you want to say? Writing will let you organise your words in effective sentences to deliver exact meaning you want to deliver.

While writing, you can imagine like you are speaking to someone, trying to explain something or develop some of your ideas. There are two parts to this exercise: first is just write as much as you can and don't stop, don't worry about how well it is written or how long your sentences are. When you are starting out, formatting and crafting perfect sentences will get you stuck. Work with quantity to get yourself comfortable writing and thinking to the paper.

Second is to format. Once your writing is done, you should read through it and see if you expressed what you wanted to express. Try to improve it, see if you can structure sentences better, if you can deliver a message with fewer words. Try to find words that will better describe your ideas and convey better meaning. Experiment with a vocabulary, it will give you flexibility in your expressions.

Exercise:

Choose any topic you like, there is a short list to help you start if your mind just gone blank.

Card games, painting, nature, technology, friendship, house animals, stars, chemistry, beer.

Now write a page about a selected topic, just let your mind flow, don't worry about delivering any message for now. It may be difficult to go past three sentences, but it will change with practice. Experiment with different topics, see what you like and try to write longer text every time. This will develop your creativity and will help you to become one of those people who can speak for ever.

Advice:

Don't worry about maintaining an original topic, if after a paragraph friendship became mathematics, it's all good, just roll with it.

Set goals and rules depending on your time and abilities. When I was experimenting with this exercise, I was writing a single page every day. It required a bit of commitment, but results were beyond what I have ever imagined.

Make it as difficult as necessary, yet as easy as it takes for you to do it.

Chapter Thirteen
Describing in detail

Your ability to describe things in great detail will improve almost every other social skill you have. Having this ability will improve stories you tell; instructions and directions you give and even express how you feel. Vague information without much detail is easy to misunderstand and you may come across as boring or like you can't be bothered to explain it well.

In many cases you will start telling a story, or a memory you will have a picture in your head and a general feel. This may make you think that you provide enough information, but while you do have an image and general feel of the incident, the person you are communicating to doesn't.

To develop our ability to effortlessly describe things, situations, and people we will need to practise building a vocabulary and a habit of grabbing and using right words. Once you have a right tool set and you know how to use it, you will be able to use it without conscious effort. In the future, even if you do just 25% you still will provide extensive information, enough for a person to form a solid understanding of whatever you are speaking about.

For this exercise you need to remember five senses hearing, seeing, touching, smelling, and feeling. Order isn't that important, but you do want to cover all of them.

Use an extensive vocabulary and experiment. You can say about a good movie: it was delicious or watching it feel like I stepped into a dog poo. Be creative and learn how to use words that you don't usually use. What you want to do is to push the line of what you are comfortable with. The further you will push yourself, the easier it will be to describe things in the future. This exercise will make your speech more interesting to listen to and will develop your ability to come up with things to say.

Exercise:

Select any random object in your field of view- spoon, fan, pen, cup, car, pants.

Start describing it in every detail using as much of your vocabulary as you can.

Repeat the process with people and situation

Advice

Set a time frame, do it for 5 or 10 minutes at the time. You probably will get out of things to say in the first minute, that was in my case. It will change with time.

Do it in your head while you are waiting in line or travelling on the bus.

Chapter Fourteen Story Preparation

Story telling is an art, this is something that will require time and practice. Your ability to tell stories well will greatly improve your social skills, charisma and variety of public speaking related activities such as presentations or simply saying a toast at friends' birthday. Ability to tell a good story can be transferred to different areas of life, you can use it to sell, convince, educate, explain and prove your point. Telling a good story is a way to deliver information in an interesting and compelling way. Stories let you take listeners on a journey and show them what you mean rather than just make a statement.

Good story will be entertaining, memorable and emotionally engaging. Best thing to do is to choose a few stories from your life, stories you enjoy the most. Prepare stories for different occasions, something funny, something dramatic and something really interesting or even hard to believe. Write them down in every detail, make sure you include emotions, sounds, smells. Your favourite stories, stories that get you emotional and take you back to the moment you experienced them are going to be the best choice, as they will naturally make you more expressive.

Use steps described below to construct your story and then practice telling it.

- Grab attention
- Set up
- Story
- Conclusion

Grab attention

Before you even start telling a story, you need to make sure that people are listening to you. Great way to grab someone's attention is to say their name. This is especially effective when you are in the group of people and everyone are speaking at the same time. If you will try to speak to everyone, no one will pay attention, because there is too much going on. Instead direct your focus towards a single person, make it personal. In many cases if one person will start listening, other will notice and will start listening as well.

Set up

This is where your story begins, but not quite yet. You want to build a story and you need a fundamental. Before you tell what has happened, you want to tell where did it happen, you want to put your story in a context. Imagine it like a movie where there is no background, and people just running in front of the green screen.

How much details to give will depend on the story, if listeners are familiar with the location, giving a name may be enough. On the other hand, if you are telling story about your trip to a place where no one has been before, providing few bright examples and drawing a picture in their head will bring your story to life.

Story

Number one task you have when telling a story is to get your listeners involved on an emotional level. What you want to do, is take listener a on a journey and let him or her feel the same thing that you have felt. The most effective way to do it is to describe how you felt when those things happened to you, how you reacted, what went through your head. If a listener can understand and relate, they will get involved on a deeper level. Be descriptive-if you felt fear, don't just say I felt fear, say I got so scared, my knees were shaking, if you got angry say: I got so angry I almost exploded. Give some extra information so your listener can understand how you felt.

Second you need to draw a picture in their heads. They haven't been there, they don't know anything, so if you don't show them, they are not going to see it. Start with the colours, it was bright sunny day, it was getting dark and street lights weren't working. Give examples or compare to something that listeners familiar with: he had the same t-shirt Jack had for his birthday.

Add sounds and smell. The more details you will give to your listener, the better picture they will form in their head. This will get them consumed and engaged. It may seem like too much, but it will take you 15 second to say it and it will make a huge difference.

Third is keep your story structured. This will make it easy to follow and to understand what is going on. It will make it easier to keep listeners attention and curiosity. Your story should flow, each sentence should serve a purpose, develop a story, help understand a situation. Get rid of fillers and distractions, that can get listeners confused. As the story progresses you want to build up tension, add mystery to what will happen.

Fourth is Conclusion, the grand finale. If it's a funny story, that's where your punch line should be, here you should sum up, bring lessons to life, make a point.

There is so many things that make a good story and only some of them are story itself. Story telling is a performance, if it is done well it is a one-person theatre, that provides listeners with a great amount of emotions. You will need to practise how to speak with emotions and express story though multiple channels. All this will come with time and practice, now however most important part is to begin.

Exercise: write three stories from your life following steps above and practice telling it.

Advice:

You can use stories to casually brag about yourself. Tell stories that will display your good qualities in a settle manner. If you tell someone a good story about how you did something courageous or funny, it will make a better impact, rather than you just saying how funny or brave you are.

Don't limit yourself to speaking, be expressive, use your hands and face to deliver a great story.

Practice telling story in front of the mirror or record a video. This may feel awkward, but it will make a huge difference.

Chapter Fifteen
Comments, Complements and Assumptions

As you have seen in examples above, there is no right and wrong here, it is all about what do you want to achieve and how comfortable you are with what you have to say. Do the exercise by steps:

Your goal

Do you want to play or speak seriously?

Think of a person

Imagine someone you know.

Select trait, quality or item they have

Think of something particular to this person, something special and personal.

Address it

Refer to chapter with preps if you need examples, but try to come up with something unique.

Follow up with a reason

This should be aligned with your goal, make it short and funny or long and sincere.

Try coming up with as many variations as you can, be creative and brave in your thinking. Try to come up with something obnoxious and over the top. Don't worry about if you will need to say it out loud, just practice coming up with as many and as fast as you can. Eventually you will find something that will work for you and along the way you will develop creativity.

Advice:

You can do this exercise in your head every time you meet someone new.

Look for opportunities to initiate body contact.

Writing will help you refine this process, but most important is to experiment.

Part 4 Big Steps

Chapter Sixteen Challenge your comfort zone

This chapter is here to take you further away from the book and inspire you to take more aggressive actions towards developing your social skills and charisma. This book should provide you with plenty of insights on what and how to do to develop your social skills and ability to never run out of things to say, without leaving your comfort zone. However, if you want to become a master of social interactions and be comfortable in any settings, with any person speaking about anything you will have to do some hard conditioning. In following chapters I will go over some of more advanced steps you can take, those will require a certain level of commitment and bravery, but look, you read the book until here, there is no reason to give up now.

Main focus of this part of the book is to expand your comfort zone, grow a thick skin and develop ability to say what you got to say without carrying what people are going to think about it. Comfort zone challenges come in various shapes and forms and their purpose is to put you in the situation where you will be not comfortable, in order for you to become comfortable in similar situations in the future. A powerful thing about it is that as you develop a bit of confidence and expand your comfort zone, it will positively influence everything that you do inside your comfort zone. It will give a serious boost to how much freedom and confidence you have in your daily life and daily interaction.

Everything that will come from this point will put you on the spot, make you a centre of attention of the group and will make you pull an entire weight of conversation alone. If those steps seem too extreme at this stage in your life, don't worry, maybe later. Think about what you can do. How can you adapt concepts of those challenges to give you results that you are looking for? For example, if public speaking is a bit too much, you can still be a centre of attention in a group of your friends. You can start preparing longer stories, practice their delivery at home and then tell them to your friends to the best of your ability. Your friends don't even have to know what you are doing; For them, it will be just a friend sharing story.

You can also easily come up with your own challenges. When I was starting out, I was doing weekly challenges that would put me in situations that I would never go through otherwise. A big part of succeeding with challenging yourself is a mindset. Commit to whatever you decide to do for a fixed amount of time and don't let lack of results affect your actions. You will progress the moment you will take the first step, but sometimes it will take a few months to see noticeable results. During this lag period, it may seem like you are wasting time, but you don't. The only way to waste time is to do nothing.

When I was starting out with comfort zone challenges, I would approach people on the street to ask for the time. I felt really stupid doing this as I had a phone in my pocket, like everyone else. I have been repeating this for one week, stopping a random person on the street to ask what time it is. Second week I started asking for time and directions. It was very awkward to ask for directions to the places I knew how to get to, but that was exactly what I was going for. To stop worrying about what I can ask or say, this was just my prejudices.

I didn't feel any confidence doing it, just awkwardness but the end of the month, I was able to give high fives to strangers on the street and recite and alphabet. This started to change my beliefs about how you should behave and what I can do. Those small victories got me into motion, gave me a habit of challenging myself as now I have proven to myself that it is possible and there is nothing to be afraid.

Your prejudices are going to be your main enemy and your mission is to face them. Once you do it a few times, you will understand that you can do more, that you are stronger than your fears and then real fun will begin.

Chapter Seventeen Public speaking

Public speaking is a major fear for many people and some rank it as close to the top as fear of death. Public speaking will let you learn some of the most important lessons when it comes to social skills and ability to deliver your ideas. Even through telling a story in front of twenty people who listen to your every word may be challenging and scary, this is exactly why you should do it.

This will:

- Greatly improve how you deliver your stories
- Improve your speech
- Develop your confidence
- Improve your body language
- Teach you how to keep people's attention

- How to speak to convince and influence

The greatest asset of public speaking is people, they will give you feedback, they will help you to improve. Amongst friends or colleges no one cares if your story sucks or if your delivery wasn't that captivating. Your friends move one and forget about it, sometimes even before you get to finish what you got to say. In those settings, you will never find out what went wrong and why did you lose the crowd. In a room with other public speakers, you will have people analysing your words and movements to give you feedback to help you grow and improve.

There is a great organisation called Toast Master, you can find in almost every large city. They are pros at turning people into public speakers. You will need to become a member to get coaching and full benefits, but you don't need to be a member if you want to give it a try. You will have a chance to give a speech in   front of a group of people, get feedback and get a general idea about what it is like to give a speech.

Another option is to search what is available in your area. You can use Google, meet up and even couch surfing to find events in your area. The good thing about doing public speaking in those settings is that the room will be filled with people who pursue the same goals as you. This will create a more friendly and non-judgmental environment. You probably will feel fear of going in front of a group of strangers, but that is a good thing; this is what will develop your confidence and inner power.

You can practise delivering a speech in the same way you practise delivering your stories, at home in front of the mirror or with a camera. However, this will not provide the same level of pressure. The goal of this chapter is to get you comfortable being exposed, comfortable with not being comfortable, and comfortable with failing. Confidence from challenging your fear will permanently change your body language, your speech and even your voice. This will make you a better speaker in daily life, someone who people will enjoy listening to.

Chapter Eighteen Improv

Improv is short for improvisation, it is a form of a life theatre where characters, plot and everything involved is improvised on the spot. Sometimes ideas for improv may come from actors or audience, but there is never any solid script, a concept or a task at most. There are few types of improv, two most common are drama and comedy. You can't lose with either one. If you have a chance, give them both a try, see what better suits your need. A big part of improv is being able to come up with a solid dialogue with a partner while you have no idea what he is thinking about or where this conversation will go. This is the perfect setting to learn how to think fast, stay present and improvise.

Good thing about the improve is that it will not be as stressful as public speaking, in a sense that you don't have to deliver alone in front of a large group of people. Most of improve done in a group, so you will always have a partner to back you up. Every class will start with a warm up, it will give you an opportunity to get out of your head and relax. Improv is incredibly fun! I did both drama and comedy improves and in both cases I had plenty of opportunities to laugh.

Usually improv classes will have around ten people. Class will start with games to get you in a mood, get your brain thinking fast and sharpen your reaction. From there, it really depends on what a teacher or a leader of the class will decide to do. I don't think I ever went to the class that didn't get ridiculous at some point, people improvise, things go sideways, you have to adapt.

From doing improv you will learn:

- How to think fast
- How to focus on the process, not on the outcome
- How to stay present
- Wit
- Creativity
- Improve your body language
- Expressiveness
- How to be comfortable in any situation
- How to be comfortable being silly

Improv is entirely based on communications between the actors and the entire conversation has to be improvised. You have to listen carefully to what your partner is saying and be fast to come up with a line that will benefit the situation. When doing improv, you will learn how important it is not to care about what others think. It will take you out of your head and will develop confidences, fast thinking and a realisation that you can say literally anything to anyone.

Finding free improv classes can be difficult, and prices will depend greatly on where you are and type of the improv. Some cities will have classes with professional teachers, some will have a bunch of armatures who just like to have fun. If you can't find anything you can always start a group and meet once a week for two to three hours. All you need is an open space and few chairs.

If you have a chance to participate in a well organised improv group, please do, as they tend to have opportunities to perform in front of the live crowd. This is never obligatory, but always a worthy experience.

Advice:

If after reading this book you are going to do only one thing – do improv. 90% of improv is your ability to think fast and say what you think, after improv you will never have a question what should I say now? It will teach you everything charismatic a person needs to know.

Chapter Nineteen Stand-up Comedy

This maybe the most challenging thing from the list, Stand Up will require preparation and organisation even before you get to go on stage, but don't let it discourage you. I can't think of anything that will make you grow a thicker skin than stand-up comedy. It perfectly combines public speaking and improvisation into a one-man performance.

Unlike public speaking and improv, doing stand-up comedy is free and, in some cases, you'll get a few drinks as well. Opportunities for gig may be hard to find and depends on where you are, bigger cities will have more options and opportunities for regular slots. During my time in UK I had to travel over an hour to a nearby city for a chance to go on stage for five minutes. Don't give up on this if you don't have it easy, it will provide you with memories for a lifetime.

Unlike with improv and public speaking you will face a crowd that cares very little about you and your feelings. This means they will judge you; They may interrupt you act with or even boo of stage, but that is extreme cases. What you need to bear in mind is that you do not want to go through these experiences, failure will give you so much more than success.

Doing stand-up, you will learn how to:

- Stay calm under pressure
- Be a centre of attention of a large crowd
- Developing a sense of humour
- Grow a thick skin
- Improvise
- Control the crowd

- Be funny and charismatic

Find your first Gig

Usually, bars will run special comedy nights, but you may find bars that just let anyone do their thing for 5 – 10 minutes. You may have a chance to preform alongside with musicians, poets or other comedians. Don't worry about that, your goal is to find a chance to go on stage and do your best to be funny and be heard. It is a good idea to book your slot few weeks in advance as they can be in demand, also the pressure of a deadline should motivate you to prepare your material.

Prepare your own material.

Writing jokes can be difficult, writing funny jokes, don't even get me started. However, I want to remind you that the most important task is to deliver material under pressure. This will develop your ability not to care what people think about you. This will give you confidence and freedom of expression and that is what you are looking for.

When it comes to writing jokes, never steal them, if you come up with a bunch of rubbish, just roll with it. In reality you can't know what is funny unless you test it. You will be surprised about what makes people laugh. Best thing to do, is to give yourself an hour or two to write without filtering or editing. Throw your mind on the paper or keyboard and after sort it out. Repeat over a period of a few days or weeks, depends on how creative you will be.

You want to go for at least 5 minutes performance first times and for five minutes you want to prepare 7 minutes of material. When you get on the stage, you are most likely to speak to fast, or simply forget some jokes. Have extra material to get you through your five minutes of fame.

Practicing

In exact same way as you did with storytelling, once you have your first 5 minutes ready - practice it. Stand up is performance, even if your jokes are funny, if you don't know how to deliver them, you will suck. Practice intonation, change your voice, move around, play with face expressions. Watch a few stand ups, you will see how much work there is behind jokes. Don't be afraid to go over the top, people laugh when things are exaggerated to ridiculous level. All this will help your goal of developing charisma.

Don't stop after you first try

First step is always the hardest, but if you want to get results you are looking for - just breaking out of your comfort zone will not be enough. You will need to learn in first person that things will be alright no matter if you will make it work or not. This means it is as important to fail as it is important to make it work. You need to develop an understanding that nothing bad will happen to you if you do something stupid and not funny in front of the large group of people. This kind of experience will bring your confidence to the level you couldn't even imagine.

In the same way you need to learn how to be funny, develop skills and understanding of what does it take to make a group of strangers laugh. And you don't have to be famous or great to make a bar laugh at your jokes. What you need is a first-person experience in failing and winning. This way you will understand that winning is not hard and failing is not dangerous.

Conclusion

Before we say our goodbye, I would like to remind you that your greatest asset in speaking with people is confidence. Don't worry about what to say, say what you want to say, say it with respect and smile.

See your social interactions like an art, preform, express and deliver. It is very easy to speak, but speaking well takes practice. I hope this book brought a better understanding on how to improve your day to day interaction and get more out of them. I am strongly convinced that social skill is one of the most valuable skills there are. Your ability to connect with people will provide you with limitless opportunities, open doors and take you on adventures. But all this is not going to happen overnight.

The only way to improve is to take real steps in the direction of your goal. Use exercises to develop your skill and craft your art.

You are rewarded in public for what you have intensely practiced & refined in private!

Tony Robins

Thank you for reading this book.

Printed in Great Britain
by Amazon